EP Language Arts 3
Printables

This book belongs to:

_____

This book was made for your convenience. It is available for printing from the Easy Peasy All-in-One Homeschool website. It contains all of the printables from Easy Peasy's Language Arts 3 course. The instructions for each page are found in the online course.

Please note, in the various places where parts of speech are practiced, certain words can be categorized in more than one place (you can go for a swim [noun] or you can swim [verb]). If your child marks one of them differently than the answer key indicates, have a conversation with them to find out why.

Easy Peasy All-in-One Homeschool is a free online homeschool curriculum providing high quality education for children around the globe. It provides complete courses for preschool through high school graduation. For EP's curriculum visit allinonehomeschool.com.

EP Language Arts 3 Printables

ISBN-13: 978-1545261170
ISBN-10: 1545261172

First Edition: May 2017

Spelling

Use the words in the box to fill in the blanks. Use each word only once.

Short a/e words		Other words		Verb spotlight
every	grand	forms	iron	solve
west	stand	near	science	solved
vest	batteries	high	school	solving
				solves

Put the <u>short a/e words</u> in alphabetical order.

_____ _____ _____

_____ _____ _____

Which of the <u>other words</u> have more than one syllable?

_____ _____

Which word is a **synonym** for *nigh*?   Which word is an **antonym** for *low*?

_____   _____

Which <u>other word</u> is plural?

_____

Write the remaining <u>other word</u>.

_____

Use a <u>verb spotlight</u> verb in a sentence that ends in a question mark.

_____

_____

Writing

Use these lines to write your poem.

_____

_____

Spelling

Use the words in the box to fill in the blanks. Use each word only once.

Short i/o/u words		Other words		Verb spotlight
slip	clog	between	motion	thump
inches	lunch	country	yard	thumped
pond	hug	plant	waves	thumping
				thumps

Put the <u>short i/o/u words</u> in alphabetical order.

_____   _____   _____

_____   _____   _____

Which of the <u>other words</u> have more than one syllable?

_____   _____   _____

Which <u>other word</u> is plural?   Write the remaining two <u>other words</u>.

_____   _____   _____

Use a <u>verb spotlight</u> verb in a sentence that ends in an exclamation point.

_____

_____

Writing

Write a color poem. Choose a color and write at least five lines.

_____

_____

_____

_____

_____

Spelling

Use the words in the box to fill in the blanks. Use each word only once.

Long a/long e words		Other words		Verb spotlight
save	easy	dresses	value	scream
sail	keep	father	area	screamed
grade	theme	pool	matter	screaming

Which of the words outside of the <u>verb spotlight</u> have more than one syllable?

_____   _____   _____

_____   _____   _____

Which of the remaining <u>long a/long e words</u> end with a silent e?

_____   _____   _____

Copy the <u>long a/e words</u> and the <u>other word</u> with a vowel pair in the middle.

_____   _____   _____

Spelling

Use the words in the box to fill in the blanks. Each word is only used once.

Long i/long o words		Other words		Verb spotlight
sign	hope	trade	current	check
tiny	stone	start	else	checked
wife	story	earth	raise	checking
				checks

Put the <u>long i/long o words</u> in alphabetical order.

_____   _____   _____

_____   _____   _____

Which of the <u>other words</u> have a sound similar to the end of *together*?

_____   _____

Which word is a **synonym** for *begin*?   Which word is an **antonym** for *lower*?

_____   _____

Which remaining <u>other word</u> has a silent e to make a long vowel sound?

_____

Write the remaining <u>other word</u>.

_____

Choose a word from the <u>verb spotlight</u> and use it in a sentence that ends in an exclamation point.

_____

_____

Spelling

Use the words in the box to fill in the blanks. Use each word only once.

st/str blend words		Other words		Verb spotlight
strong	least	upon	base	reach
strip	burst	next	expand	reached
stream	east	own	calculate	reaching
				reaches

Which of the other words have more than one syllable?

_____   _____   _____

Which of the blend words have three consonants in a row?

_____   _____   _____

_____

Which of the remaining words start with a vowel?

_____   _____

Put the remaining words outside of the verb spotlight in alphabetical order.

_____   _____   _____

Use one verb spotlight verb in a sentence that ends in a period and another in a sentence that ends in a question mark.

_____

_____

_____

Spelling

Use the words in the box to fill in the blanks. Use each word only once.

kn/wr words		Other words		Verb spotlight
known	wrong	while	sum	think
knock	wrist	product	digit	thought
knife	wrinkle	subtract	round	thinking
				thinks

Which of the other words are math words?

_____   _____   _____

_____   _____

Which of the remaining words have a silent e?

_____   _____   _____

Which word is a synonym for *incorrect*?   Which is an antonym for *unknown*?

_____   _____

The two remaining words both have a silent letter. Write the words here:

_____   _____

Use one verb spotlight verb in a sentence that includes a pronoun.

_____

_____

Spelling

Use the words in the box to fill in the blanks. Use each word only once.

gh/ph words		Other words		Verb spotlight
bought	graph	along	lady	break
laughed	paragraph	close	seem	broke
enough	photograph	something	street	breaking
				breaks

Which of the words outside of the <u>verb spotlight</u> have more than one syllable?

_____ _____ _____

_____ _____ _____

Which of the <u>gh/ph words</u> are in the past tense?

_____ _____

Which word is a homophone for *seam*?   Which is an antonym for *open*?

_____   _____

Write the two remaining words that aren't in the <u>verb spotlight</u> list.

_____ _____

Use one <u>verb spotlight</u> verb in a question.

_____

_____

Spelling

Use the words in the box to fill in the blanks. Use each word only once.

ch/tch words		Other words		Verb spotlight
chance	match	front	difference	open
choose	batch	safe	property	opened
child	watch	whole	travel	opening
				opens

Put the ch/tch words in alphabetical order.

_____   _____   _____

_____   _____   _____

Which of the other words have three syllables?

_____   _____

Which word is a synonym for *journey*?   Which is an antonym for *back*?

_____   _____

Which of the other words have a silent e?

_____   _____

Use one verb spotlight verb in a command.

_____

_____

Spelling

Use the words in the box to fill in the blanks. Use each word only once.

Soft g words		Other words		Verb spotlight
giraffe	stage	paper	children	push
gentle	engine	mirror	ocean	pushed
ginger	badge	reflect	fraction	pushing
				pushes

Put the <u>other words</u> in alphabetical order.

_____   _____   _____

_____   _____   _____

Which <u>soft g words</u> have one syllable?

_____   _____

Which <u>soft g words</u> have a *short e* sound?

_____   _____

Which remaining <u>soft g word</u> has a silent e that does *not* make the vowel sound long?

_____

Write the remaining word from the <u>soft g words</u> list.

_____

Use a <u>verb spotlight</u> verb in a sentence that ends in an exclamation point.

_____

_____

Spelling

Use the words in the box to fill in the blanks. Use each word only once.

oi sound words		Other words		Verb spotlight
choice	royal	group	otter	walk
voice	annoy	oddly	forest	walked
noise	destroy	night	equation	walking
				walks

Which oi sound words have more than one syllable?

_____ _____ _____

Which oi sound words have a *silent e*?

_____ _____ _____

Which other words have a *short o* sound?

_____ _____

Which other words have a different o sound?

_____ _____

Which other word is an antonym for *day*?

_____

Which other word helps you solve a math problem?

_____

Use a verb spotlight verb in a sentence that contains a quotation.

_____

_____

Spelling

Use the words in the box to fill in the blanks. Use each word only once.

ou sound words		Other words		Verb spotlight
shouted	crown	desert	began	take
around	growl	important	river	took
pounds	however	sea	influence	taking
				takes

Which <u>other words</u> have more than one syllable?

_____   _____   _____

_____   _____

Which <u>ou sound word</u> is past tense?   Which <u>ou sound word</u> is plural?

_____   _____

Which word is a synonym for ocean? Which <u>ou sound word</u> has three syllables?

_____   _____

Which remaining words outside of the <u>verb spotlight</u> have only one syllable?

_____   _____

Write the last word outside of the <u>verb spotlight</u>.

_____

Use a <u>verb spotlight</u> verb in a sentence that contains a list with commas.

_____

_____

Helping Verbs

Circle the letter next to the helping verb that correctly completes the sentence.

Amy, Laura, and I ___ going to the mall.

a.   are
b.   is
c.   am

Laura ____ asking her mom to drive us.

a.   are
b.   is
c.   am

We ____ look for new shoes for our dance class.

a.   will
b.   had
c.   have

I ____ hoping to find some with sparkles and a strap.

a.   are
b.   is
c.   am

We _____ enjoying our dance class this year.

a.   have been
b.   has been
c.   will be

Spelling

Use the words in the box to fill in the blanks. Use each word only once.

Short aw words		Other words		Verb spotlight
crawl	pause	sleep	once	carry
dawn	author	resemble	disappear	carried
paws	laundry	polygon	north	carrying
				carries

Put the other words in alphabetical order.

_____   _____   _____

_____   _____   _____

Which two short aw words are homophones of each other?

_____   _____

Which remaining short aw words only have one vowel?

_____   _____

Which short aw word is a synonym for writer?

_____

Write the last word that isn't a part of the verb spotlight.

_____

Use a verb spotlight verb in a sentence that ends with a question mark.

_____

_____

Spelling

Use the words in the box to fill in the blanks. Use each word only once.

long/short oo words		Other words		Verb spotlight
loose	shook	pentagon	shock	crash
balloon	looked	south	second	crashed
goose	understood	those	predict	crashing
				crashes

Which words outside of the <u>verb spotlight</u> have more than one syllable?

_____   _____   _____

_____   _____

Which words outside of the <u>verb spotlight</u> end in a *silent e*?

_____   _____   _____

Which word is a direction?

_____

Which remaining words start with the consonant blend *sh*?

_____   _____

Which remaining <u>long/short oo word</u> is past tense?

_____

Use a <u>verb spotlight</u> verb in a sentence that ends with an exclamation point.

_____

_____

Adjectives

Underline the adjective that best completes the sentence. Both choices are adjectives, but which one better describes the noun?

The deck was _____ after the rain. (soaked/scratchy)

The phone was _____ with the ringer all the way up. (purple/loud)

Jane's _____ blue eyes sparkled as she smiled. (angry/beautiful)

It was _____ news that our lost dog had returned. (thrilling/tasty)

The _____ painting was hanging in a museum. (large/energetic)

Dinner last night was _____. (bright/delicious)

The _____ wind blew the trees as the storm raged. (harsh/fluffy)

The video game was _____. (brown/exciting)

Write in an adjective that fits with the sentence. Be as descriptive as you can.

The bird flew in a _____ line.

The gravel road felt really _____.

Our _____ driveway fits two cars.

The math whiz was incredibly _____.

Spelling

Use the words in the box to fill in the blanks. Use each word only once.

air sound words		Other words		Verb spotlight
stairs	glare	almost	buy	miss
repair	compare	Indian	real	missed
airplane	prepare	among	quadrilateral	missing
				misses

Put the air sound words in alphabetical order.

_____   _____   _____

_____   _____   _____

Which other word is a proper noun?

_____

Which word is a synonym for *not quite*?   Which is an antonym for *fake*?

_____   _____

Which word has five syllables?   Which word can relate to money?

_____   _____

Write the remaining other word.

_____

Use a verb spotlight verb in a descriptive sentence with at least one adjective.

_____

_____

Adjectives and Antonyms

Read each sentence and underline the adjective. Then rewrite the sentence using the antonym or opposite of the adjective from the word box. For example, if the original sentence was *The windows are not clean*, *clean* would be the adjective and *dirty* would be its antonym. Your new sentence would be *The windows are dirty*.

cold	loud	down	wet	fast	happy
long	hard	young	broken		

This book is not short. _____

My brother is not quiet. _____

Our radio is not functional. _____

That race was not slow. _____

The girl is not sad. _____

The man is not old. _____

The air is not warm. _____

The sun is not up. _____

The concrete is not soft. _____

The towel is not dry. _____

Spelling

Use the words in the box to fill in the blanks. Use each word only once.

Homophones		Other words		Verb spotlight
here	hear	young	morning	fly
bear	bare	pulled	angles	flew
way	weigh	magnify	cone	flying
				flies

Which <u>other words</u> have more than one syllable?

_____   _____   _____

Which of the <u>homophones</u> means *this place*?   Which can mean *listen*?

_____   _____

Which of the <u>homophones</u> is an animal?   Which means *naked*?

_____   _____

Which of the <u>homophones</u> can tell where to go?   Which finds out *how heavy*?

_____   _____

Which <u>other word</u> is past tense?

_____

Write the remaining two <u>other words</u>.

_____   _____

Use a <u>verb spotlight</u> verb in a sentence that ends with an exclamation point.

_____

_____

Adjectives and Synonyms

Read each sentence and underline the adjective. Then rewrite the sentence using the **synonym** or similar word for the adjective from the word box. For example, if the original sentence was *The windows are dirty*, *dirty* would be the adjective and *filthy* could be a synonym. Your new sentence would be *The windows are filthy*.

freezing	noisy	fantastic	soaked	quick
delighted	lengthy	scratchy	delicious	glistening

This road is long. _____

My music is loud. _____

The road is wet. _____

That car was fast. _____

The baby is happy. _____

It is cold outside. _____

The sandpaper is rough. _____

That concert was excellent! _____

The snack was yummy. _____

The shiny diamond sparkled. _____

Spelling

Use the words in the box to fill in the blanks. Use each word only once.

Homophones		Other words		Verb spotlight
flower	flour	sugar	it's	smell
bored	board	being	orbit	smelled
hair	hare	leave	position	smelling
				smells

Which other words have more than one syllable?

_____   _____   _____

_____

Which of the homophones is a plant?   Which is a bread ingredient?

_____   _____

Which of the homophones means *uninterested*?   Which is a plank of wood?

_____   _____

Which of the homophones grows on your head?   Which is a rabbit?

_____   _____

Which other word is a contraction?   Which is a synonym of *depart*?

_____   _____

Use a verb spotlight verb in a sentence that ends with an exclamation point.

_____

_____

Describe with Adjectives

Study this picture. Then use descriptive words to explain what you see. Be specific! Read your description to a family member and see if they can draw what you have described. What could you change to make your description even more specific?

_____

_____

_____

_____

_____

_____

Spelling

Use the words in the box to fill in the blanks. Use each word only once.

ur sound words		Other words		Verb spotlight
curled	firm	polygon	clear	visit
church	skirt	experiment	noun	visited
perfect	person	cylinder	verb	visiting
				visits

Put the <u>ur sound words</u> in alphabetical order.

_____   _____   _____

_____   _____   _____

Which word has four syllables?

_____

Which <u>other words</u> are shapes?

_____   _____

Which <u>other words</u> are parts of speech?

_____   _____

Write the remaining <u>other word</u>.

_____

Use a <u>verb spotlight</u> verb in a question that contains adjectives.

_____

_____

Adjectives and Nouns

In each sentence, underline the adjective. Then on the line beside the sentence, write the noun that is being described by the adjective.

I wore an itchy sweater to school.   _____

My sister wants a miniature pony.   _____

The wild animals made some noise.   _____

The noisy kids sounded like animals.   _____

The delicious candy is gone.   _____

Our church has an expensive piano.   _____

The colorful robe is on the hanger.   _____

My mom has such beautiful eyes.   _____

My aunt has long hair.   _____

The movie was boring.   _____

My brother is sick.   _____

Spelling

Use the words in the box to fill in the blanks. Use each word only once.

Double consonant words		Other words		Verb spotlight
hugged	happy	evidence	burned	talk
correct	different	opinion	conduct	talked
funny	error	likely	certain	talking
				talks

Which <u>double consonant words</u> have two syllables?

_____   _____   _____

_____

Which <u>double consonant word</u> has one syllable?   Which has three syllables?

_____   _____

Which <u>other words</u> start with a vowel?

_____   _____

Which <u>other word</u> starts with a *hard* c?   Which starts with a *soft* c?

_____   _____

Which word is a synonym for *probable*?   Which is in the past tense?

_____   _____

Use a <u>verb spotlight</u> verb in a statement.

_____

_____

Summary

Read the short story by Jenn Appel below and then summarize it. Write the main idea of the story in the big oval with supporting ideas in the ovals below it.

The only thing Bristol had in mind that morning when she woke was going sledding. She rushed to do her morning chores – washing dishes, picking up her room, cleaning off the table, and starting laundry. She made quick work of all her jobs before begging her mother to go sledding.

Her mother was thrilled to see Bristol had finished all her chores without having to be told. She told her to get ready to sled. Bristol put on her snow pants, boots, coat, gloves, and hat. She grabbed her orange sled, and the two of them walked hand in hand towards the hill, both happy for the beautiful day ahead of them.

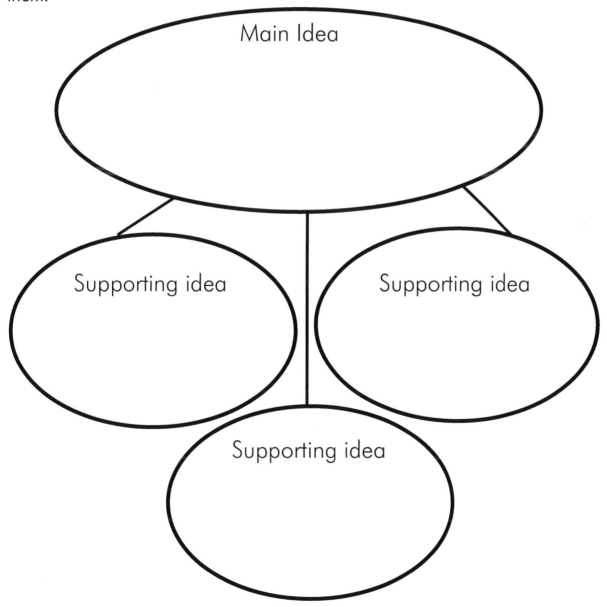

Main Idea

Supporting idea

Supporting idea

Supporting idea

Adjectives and Nouns

In each sentence, underline the adjective. Then on the line beside the sentence, write the noun that is being described by the adjective.

The giant spider scared me.   _____

My dad takes me on big adventures.   _____

The exotic bird was squawking.   _____

The blonde woman left her purse.   _____

The gray clouds gave way to rain.   _____

The hungry cat waited for his food.   _____

The bouncy ball hit the ceiling.   _____

My favorite shoes are missing.   _____

My dog is so fluffy after his bath.   _____

Our mailman is very friendly.   _____

The fussy baby woke me up.   _____

Writing

Write a postcard. Where are you writing from? Home? The moon? Somewhere else?

Spelling

Use the words in the box to fill in the blanks. Use each word only once.

Compound words		Other words		Verb spotlight
notebook	football	future	sphere	sing
bookcase	hallway	forecast	highest	sang
classroom	outdoors	conclusion	pyramid	singing
				sings

Put the <u>compound words</u> in alphabetical order.

_____ _____ _____

_____ _____ _____

Which <u>other words</u> have three syllables?

_____ _____

Which unused <u>other word</u> is a shape?   Which can be a weather word?

_____   _____

Which word is a synonym for *upcoming*?   Which is a synonym for *utmost*?

_____   _____

Use a <u>verb spotlight</u> verb in a statement and another in a question.

_____

_____

_____

_____

Story Summary

Read the following short story by Jenn Appel. Then write a summary of the story.

Do you know what the fastest animal in the world is? If you answered cheetah, you're right. However, a cheetah can only run quickly for less than half of a mile before being too exhausted to continue. If a cheetah were in a mile-long race, it would lose to a pronghorn.

A pronghorn is sometimes mistaken for an antelope but is more related to the goat family. These unique animals can sustain speeds of around thirty miles an hour for twenty miles! Try to get a cheetah to do that, and you'll be quickly disappointed.

Next time someone asks you to run like a cheetah, remember the pronghorn and try to run like it instead.

What is the **main idea** of the story? Write one complete sentence that tells the story's main idea.

_____

_____

What are the **most important things** that happened in the story? Write one or two complete sentences that tell the story's most important things.

_____

_____

_____

Story Summary

Read this short story. Then write a summary of the story.

A unique type of cloud, the lenticular cloud, is frequently mistaken for a UFO. These special clouds form above a mountain, a tall building, or other large object that can obstruct air flow. A slight wind creates waves on the side of the object opposite the direction of the wind. Given the right temperatures, the moisture in the air condenses to produce a strange, saucer-shaped cloud. Lenticular clouds can actually be quite dangerous for pilots of powered aircraft due to the turbulence created above them. Interestingly though, glider pilots use the turbulence to their advantage. In fact, the world records for both distance and altitude of a glider were set utilizing the turbulence of lenticular clouds.

What is the **main idea** of the story? Write one complete sentence that tells the story's main idea.

_____

_____

What are the **most important things** that happened in the story? Write one or two complete sentences that tell the story's most important things.

_____

_____

_____

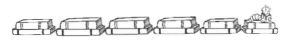

Story Summary

Read this abridged Aesop's Fable, "The Fox and the Crow." Write a summary.

One bright morning as the Fox was following his sharp nose through the wood in search of a bite to eat, he saw a Crow on the limb of a tree overhead. This lucky Crow held a bit of cheese in her beak.

"No need to search any farther," thought sly Master Fox. "Here is a dainty bite for my breakfast."

Up he trotted to the foot of the tree in which the Crow was sitting, and looking up admiringly, he cried, "Good-morning, beautiful creature!"

The Crow, her head cocked on one side, watched the Fox suspiciously. But she kept her beak tightly closed on the cheese and did not return his greeting.

"What a charming creature she is!" said the Fox. "How her feathers shine! What a beautiful form and what splendid wings! Could she sing just one song, I know I should hail her Queen of Birds."

Listening to these flattering words, the Crow forgot all her suspicion, and also her breakfast. She wanted very much to be called Queen of Birds.

So she opened her beak wide to utter her loudest caw, and down fell the cheese straight into the Fox's open mouth.

_____

_____

_____

_____

_____

Story Summary

Read this Greek myth. Then write a summary of what you read.

Daedalus was an architect and inventor. His son was Icarus. They lived on the Isle of Crete but wished to return to their home in Athens. Being a fabulous inventor, Daedalus created a pair of artificial wings that allowed Icarus and himself to fly. He made the wings out of feathers held tightly together by wax.

As they began their journey home, Daedalus warned Icarus not to fly too high. This would cause him to get too close to the sun, melting the wax that held his wings together. Unfortunately, Icarus ignored his father's instructions. His wings melted and he plummeted into the Mediterranean Sea.

_____

_____

_____

_____

Spelling

Use the words in the box to fill in the blanks. Use each word only once.

-ful/-fully words		Other words		Verb spotlight
beautiful	thankfully	feature	basket	empty
cheerful	joyfully	history	welcome	emptied
useful	helpfully	advantage	until	emptying
				empties

Which words outside of the <u>verb spotlight</u> have three syllables?

_____   _____   _____

_____   _____   _____

Which remaining words outside of the <u>verb spotlight</u> start with a vowel?

_____   _____

Which word is a synonym for *happy*?   Which word can mean *aspect*?

_____   _____

Which word can be a greeting?   Which word is a container?

_____   _____

Use a <u>verb spotlight</u> verb in a dialogue with two quotation sentences.

_____

_____

_____

Main Idea and Details

Read the paragraphs and answer the questions about them.

Main ideas are what the paragraph or story is about. Sometimes they are stated (usually in the first sentence of a paragraph). Sometimes they are unstated and are more of a summary of the whole paragraph.

What is the main idea of this paragraph?
    a. Sometimes main ideas are stated.
    b. Main ideas are what the paragraph or story is about.
    c. Sometimes main ideas are unstated.

Emma, Miley, and Kara had a fun day at the pool. They played water polo while giggling and splashing. They did flips off of the diving board. They laid out in the warm sun to soak up the vitamin D. They were glad for a day of fun in the sun.

What is the main idea of this paragraph?
    a. Emma, Miley, and Kara had a fun day at the pool.
    b. They played water polo while giggling and splashing.
    c. They laid out in the warm sun.

Why did they lay out in the warm sun?
    a. They were glad for a day of fun in the sun.
    b. They wanted to soak up the vitamin D.
    c. They wanted to have a fun day at the pool.

Fruits and vegetables have lots of vitamins and minerals. They can boost your immune system and help you avoid sickness. They increase energy and leave you feeling alert.

What is the main idea of this paragraph?
    a. Fruits and vegetables have lots of vitamins and minerals.
    b. They increase energy and leave you feeling alert.
    c. There are many benefits to fruits and vegetables.

Why do fruits and vegetables leave you feeling alert?
    a. They have lots of vitamins and minerals.
    b. They increase energy.
    c. They can boost your immune system.

Spelling

Use the words in the box to fill in the blanks. Use each word only once.

Contractions		Other Words		Verb Spotlight
didn't	haven't	natural	pretty	pass
you're	she's	climate	cycle	passed
we're	they're	federal	lunar	passing
				passes

Put the <u>other words</u> in alphabetical order.

_____   _____   _____

_____   _____   _____

Which contractions stand for a pair of words with *not* in them?

_____   _____

Which contractions stand for a pair of words with *are* in them?

_____   _____   _____

Which contraction stands for a pair of words with *is* in them?

_____

Use a <u>verb spotlight</u> verb in an exclamation and a statement.

_____

_____

_____

Adjectives and Nouns

In each sentence, fill in the blank with an adjective that fits the sentence. Then underline the noun being described.

The shirt that I wore was _____.

The dishes on the counter are _____.

The ring on her finger was _____.

The girl's hair was _____.

The cake was _____.

She had _____ gum stuck in her hair.

The _____ water refreshed the athletes.

The _____ crash startled them all.

His _____ nose needs a tissue.

The cantata was _____.

My dog looks _____.

Comparative Adjectives

Adjectives that are used to compare two things are called **comparative adjectives**. *Smarter, more colorful, happier,* and *less* are all examples of comparative adjectives. Write the comparative form of the following adjectives:

peaceful _____   clean   _____

crazy   _____   excited _____

young   _____   strong _____

angry   _____   happy   _____

quiet   _____   wet   _____

green   _____   scared _____

big   _____   brave   _____

bad   _____   far   _____

silly   _____   good   _____

dirty   _____   pretty _____

easy   _____   healthy _____

boring _____   friendly _____

sweet   _____   safe   _____

high   _____   thin   _____

busy   _____   short   _____

large   _____   dry   _____

early   _____   hot   _____

Superlative Adjectives

Adjectives that are used to show the highest or lowest ranking among things are called **superlative adjectives**. *Smartest, most colorful, happiest,* and *least* are all examples of superlative adjectives. Write the superlative form of the following adjectives:

careful	_____	dirty	_____
scary	_____	curious	_____
old	_____	cold	_____
sad	_____	dry	_____
long	_____	red	_____
curly	_____	close	_____
thin	_____	quiet	_____
excited	_____	large	_____
good	_____	happy	_____
easy	_____	bad	_____
pretty	_____	busy	_____
big	_____	early	_____
sweet	_____	far	_____
silly	_____	scared	_____
brave	_____	friendly	_____
high	_____	young	_____

Comparative or Superlative

For each sentence, fill in the **comparative** (comparing two things) or **superlative** (highest or lowest rank among a series of things) form of the adjective in the blank. The last one is tricky. Can you figure it out?

My dad is __(strong)__ than yours. _____

Your sister is the __(happy)__ little girl. _____

Jeff is __(hungry)__ than James. _____

Canada is __(peaceful)__ than Syria. _____

Her feet are the __(small)__ I've seen. _____

My room is __(clean)__ than yours. _____

That's the __(big)__ snowball ever. _____

The last clown was the __(silly)__ . _____

Her hair is the __(beautiful)__ of all. _____

The earth is __(small)__ than Jupiter. _____

The swings are __(fun)__ than the slide. _____

Rhode Island is the __(small)__ state. _____

Her score was the __(good)__ all year. _____

Paragraph Writing

Use the hamburger below to help you write a paragraph. Today, come up with your main idea and two supporting details for that main idea. You will complete this in lesson 129.

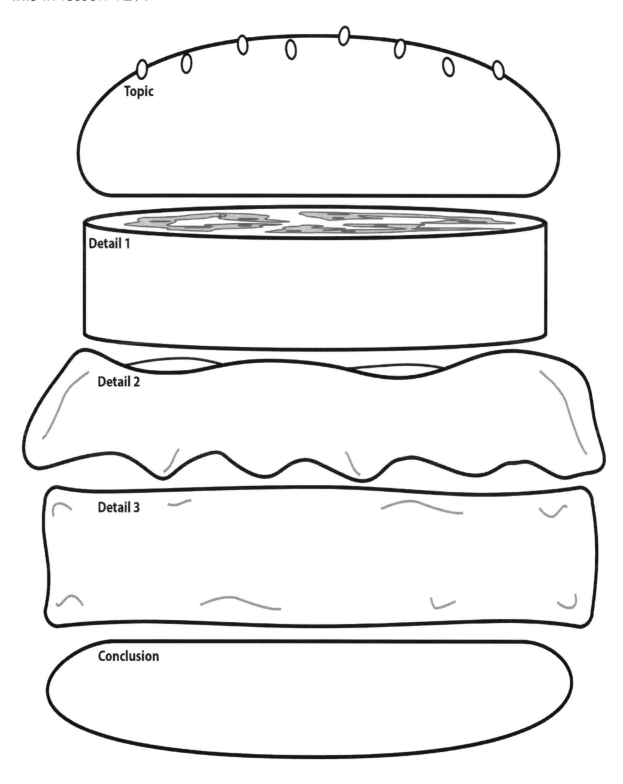

Topic

Detail 1

Detail 2

Detail 3

Conclusion

Comparative and Superlative Adjectives

In each sentence, underline the comparative or superlative adjective. Then on the line beside the sentence, write the things that are being compared.

She was the prettiest girl in school. _____

The doll was bigger than the teacup. _____

July was the hottest month of the year. _____

Friday was colder than Saturday. _____

The rose is the most beautiful flower. _____

Water is more beneficial than soda. _____

It was the longest book I've ever read. _____

Black is darker than pink. _____

Your car is faster than mine. _____

My grandpa's car is the slowest. _____

My dog's hair is fluffiest after a bath. _____

Paragraph Writing

Fill in this hamburger for a paragraph summary of a chapter you've read. What's the topic, or main idea, of the chapter? You will have a topic or main idea sentence, three supporting detail sentences, and a closing sentence about the topic. Can you use at least one compound sentence?

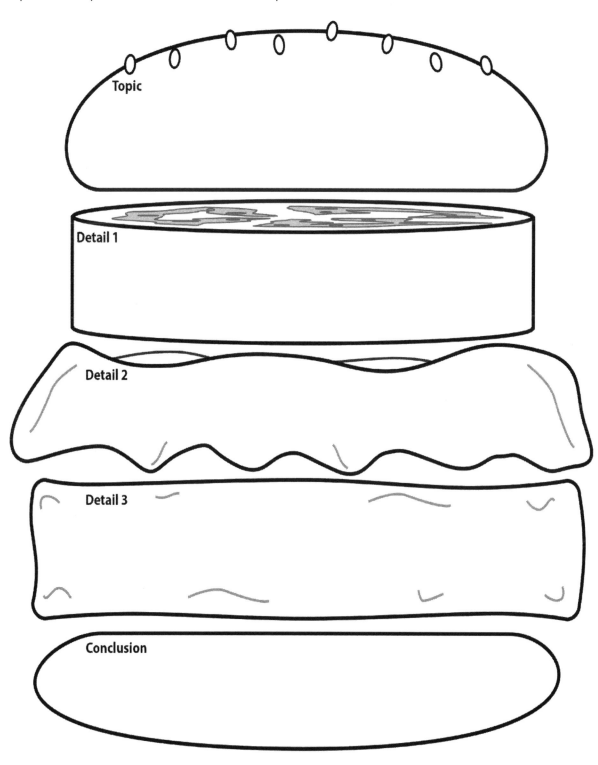

Topic

Detail 1

Detail 2

Detail 3

Conclusion

Spelling

Use the words in the box to fill in the blanks. Use each word only once.

-er words		Other words		Verb spotlight
under	fever	state	main	dance
whether	never	interaction	explorer	danced
answer	border	swim	prior	dancing
				dances

Put the <u>other words</u> in alphabetical order.

_____   _____   _____

_____   _____   _____

Which <u>–er word</u> is an antonym for *always*?   Which is a synonym for *beneath*?

_____   _____

Which <u>–er word</u> is a homophone of *weather*?   Which can mean *reply*?

_____   _____

Which <u>–er word</u> can indicate sickness?   Write the last <u>–er word</u>.

_____   _____

Use a <u>verb spotlight</u> verb in two statements that include adjectives.

_____

_____

_____

_____

Spelling

Use the words in the box to fill in the blanks. Use each word only once.

-le/-al words		Other words		Verb spotlight
total	chuckle	infer	knowledge	wrap
signal	giggle	modify	sequence	wrapped
central	candle	doesn't	comprehend	wrapping
				wraps

Put the -le/-al words in alphabetical order.

_____   _____   _____

_____   _____   _____

Which other words have three syllables?

_____   _____

Which other word is a contraction?   Which means *assume*?

_____   _____

Which other word is a synonym for *order*?   Which can mean *intelligence*?

_____   _____

Use a verb spotlight verb in a statement and question that each use a quotation.

_____

_____

_____

Simple, Compound, and Complex Sentences

Make **compound sentences** using *and*, *but*, *or*. Use each conjunction once to combine the given sentences with another sentence that you create.

The dress is pretty. _____

_____

The dog is muddy. _____

_____

Should I eat this cold soup? _____

_____

Make **complex sentences** by adding each of *when*, *if*, *because* to make these sentences longer by adding a **clause**, a group of words with a subject and verb.

The phone rang, but we didn't hear it. _____

_____

I like lettuce, and I like tomatoes, too. _____

_____

We can watch a movie. _____

_____

Conjunctions

Combine the sentences using one of the **conjunctions** or joining words below.
There can be more than one answer, so try to use a different word each time.

and	if	or	because	since	but

We went to the bank. Then we went to the store.

_____

_____

I like pizza. It tastes good.

_____

Wear your gloves and hat. It is cold outside.

_____

_____

You can have an apple. You can have an orange.

_____

_____

She won first place. She was the best runner.

_____

_____

He wished he could have gone. He was sick.

_____

_____

A Caterpillar's Voice

Circle the letter that best completes the word in the sentence.

A frightening animal was in the ___are's den.   **h sc bl**

The animal's voice ___ared out.   **h sc bl**

All of the other animals were ___ared.   **h sc bl**

Fill in the blanks with words from the word box to complete the story.

day	cave	brave	scary
	saving	afraid	

A caterpillar crawled into the hare's _____.

He used the echo in the cave to make himself sound

like a big, _____ animal. All of the other

animals were _____ to go into the cave. The

frog, though, was very _____. He ended

up _____ the _____.

Final Project

Fill in the sections below on character, setting, and plot.

Who are your **characters**? Write them here:

_____

_____

_____

What is your **setting**? Where and when does your play take place? Will there be other settings? Write them here:

_____

_____

_____

What is your **plot**? What are some problems your characters will face? Write them here:

_____

_____

_____

Final Project

Fill in this story map with information about your **plot**.

Problem

Beginning: What is going to create the problem?

_____

_____

_____

_____

Middle: How are they going to try to solve the problem and fail? What other problems are going to make it worse?

_____

_____

_____

_____

_____

_____

End: How will the problem be solved?

_____

_____

_____

Final Project

Today you will learn about revising your play.

Ask yourself the following questions:

In the **beginning of the play**:

- Did I talk about the **setting**? Did I tell the reader where and when the story takes place?

- Did I show the **main problem** of the play? Will a reader understand what the problem was?

In the **middle of the play**:

- Did some of my **characters** try to solve the **main problem**? What happened when they tried? Was it clear?

How would I describe the **end of my play**? Circle a choice:

happy   funny   sad   surprising   something else: _____

After you ask yourself these questions, perform these proofreading steps:

- Check that each word is spelled correctly. Look it up if you're not sure.
- Check that each sentence starts with a capital letter and ends with proper punctuation.
- Don't be afraid to ask for help!

If you want to make any changes to your story, do it during the revision process. Think of a change that might make your story more exciting, fun, or interesting. Describe it on the lines below.

_____

_____

Made in the USA
Coppell, TX
22 July 2020